AngularJs vs EmberJs

a guide to choosing your single
page application framework

Brendan Graetz

AngularJs vs EmberJs

a guide to choosing your single page application framework

Brendan Graetz

This book is for sale at
http://leanpub.com/angularjs-emberjs-compare

This version was published on 2015-10-17

ISBN 978-1518664083

Tweet This Book!

Please help Brendan Graetz by spreading the word about this book on Twitter!

The suggested tweet for this book is:

I just bought #AngularjsVsEmberjs by @bguiz on Leanpub

The suggested hashtag for this book is #AngularjsVsEmberjs.

Find out what other people are saying about the book by clicking on this link to search for this hashtag on Twitter:

https://twitter.com/search?q=#AngularjsVsEmberjs

Contents

AngularJs vs EmberJs

So you want to start building a single-page application. Which framework should you use to help build it?

AngularJs vs EmberJs

This series of articles takes a look at two of the most popular ones: AngularJs[1] and EmberJs[2]

---

[1]http://angularjs.org/
[2]http://emberjs.com/

The back story

While developing applications using BackboneJs, I have been itching to use a newer JavaScript single-page application (SPA) framework; if at least to find out if it was indeed worth continuing to develop with the tried-and-tested, battle proven, but often verbose and feature lacking, BackboneJs[3].

At first, I had wanted to compare all the SPAs.

Learn All the SPAs!

However, that meant I would be spreading myself too thin. Besides, we already have TodoMVC[4] for that.

What I really wanted to do was to take the two most popular SPAs after BackboneJs, and analyse them in depth - pitting them against each other, and taking a look at the pros and cons of each.

[3]http://backbonejs.org/
[4]http://todomvc.com/

Given that they both fall into the same broad category, and are designed to help developers accomplish similar end goals, I expected them to be quite similar.

Interestingly, they were not. It was not just the syntax that was different. I found that they have very different philosophies on how code should be structured, and even how much structure there should be; making for quite an interesting comparison.

Let us take a look!

Editions

The **online edition** of this book is available at angularjs-emberjs-compare.bguiz.com[5].

The **PDF, ePub, and Mobi editions** of this book are available at Leanpub[6].

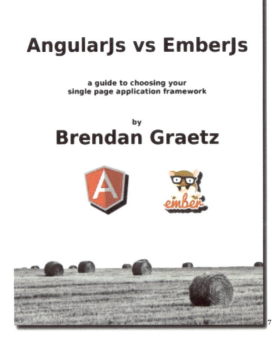

If you liked this book, and wish to support it, please purchase a copy on Leanpub. 10% of proceeds are donated to the Electronic Frontier Foundation[8]. The online edition of this

---

[5]http://angularjs-emberjs-compare.bguiz.com

[6]https://leanpub.com/angularjs-emberjs-compare?a=27hVMyWVn46xaZCi6E563X&subID=gitbookb

[7]https://leanpub.com/angularjs-emberjs-compare?a=27hVMyWVn46xaZCi6E563X&subID=gitbookbc

[8]https://www.eff.org/

book is free, and will always remain free.

Author

Brendan Graetz tries almost every new programming language, when it comes out, for fun.

He has been building production software using NodeJs on the back end and Javascript on the front end. Most of his code adventures are catalogued at blog.bguiz.com[9] where you can check out his other writing.

You can connect with him on Twitter twitter.com/bguiz[10]:

... and on Github github.com/bguiz[11]

... and on LinkedIn[12]

---

[9]http://blog.bguiz.com

[10]https://twitter.com/bguiz

[11]https://github.com/bguiz

[12]https://www.linkedin.com/in/brendangraetz

Criteria

I would like to kick off this series of articles by defining what exactly we will be comparing, when comparing AngularJs to EmberJs.

The space that these two operate in - JavaScript frameworks used to develop single-page applications - is a rather complex one. It is complex because of the number of different issues, concepts, and even philosophies, that SPAs touch. Furthermore, this area is a moving target, because SPAs are a fairly new thing, and still going through the initial stages of rapid development.

Thus, the only certainty here is that there is no definitive answer. We shall try, nonetheless.

Why criteria are necessary

Without facts, opinions will have their day in the park. We want to make this as **objective** as possible.

Also it helps you, the reader, know if this series of articles is going to be worth your time reading.

If - and I know this is a *silly* example - the better logo is of utmost importance, and you wish to choose your framework based on that; then these articles are *not* for you, because you will not see this being listed as one of the criteria below.

That being said, if I have missed out on something out below, and you think it would benefit the discussion, let me know[13], or submit a pull request[14].

---

[13]https://twitter.com/bguiz
[14]https://github.com/bguiz/angular-ember-compare

What the criteria are

- Learning curve
- Models
- Views
- Controllers
- Router
- Templating
- Components
- Dependency management
- Build tooling
- Opinionation
- Development tooling
- Dependencies
- Community
- Track record
- Contributions
- Maturity
- Level of abstraction/ structure
- Testability

There we have it, all the criteria that this series of articles will cover!

A note on fairness and polarisation

Which one is better at what?

One framework is going to better than the other on some things, and the other way around on the others.

It is worth pointing out here that this a fairly polarised topic, with the communities of developers using each of these frameworks, firmly believing that their framework of choice is the best thing since sliced bread (or at least **way better** than the other).

Thus I feel that it is necessary to do a little bit of a **disclaimer** here, and state that I belong to neither camp. I have worked with jQuery mobile, and BackboneJs before; and have also been keeping abreast with both AngularJs and EmberJs, but have not developed anything more complex than a Todo application[15].

tl;dr= I am going to be fair and unbiased.

---

[15]http://todomvc.com

Questions

For each of the criteria, here are the main questions that we will be taking a look at:

Learning curve

- How fast can you get going and get productive with the framework?
- Can you get by with Google and Stackoverflow?
- Do you need to take a course to learn it?
- How does this change as the application gets more complex?

Models

- What syntax is used to express models?
- What additional libraries do you need to use models?
- How easy is it to get/ sync models between client and server?

Views

- What syntax is used to express views?
- How do they interact with the controllers, models, and router?

Controllers

- What syntax is used to express controllers?
- Declarative or imperative?
- Support for two-way data binding, between the models and views?

Router

- What syntax is used to express a router?
- Does the router support flat or hierarchical routes?
- What additional libraries do you need to use the router?

Templating

- What is the templating syntax?
- Declarative or imperative?
- What additional libraries are used?
- Are the templates string based or DOM based?
- Are the templates easy to work with for designers who are not developers?

Components

- What syntax is used to express a component?
- What level of abstraction do these components sit at?
- How well do these components align with the current draft specification for web components?

Dependency management

- What syntax or convention is used to express that one module depends upon another?
- Does the framework encourage modular development to begin with?
- How robust is this means of managing dependencies between modules?

Build tooling

- What build tools exist to build an application using each framework?
- What limitations do the current build tools have, and what are they good at?
- What future build tools are in the pipeline?

Opinionation

- How opinionated is the framework with regards to how to develop an application?
- How does this opinionation benefit and detract from the framework?

Development tooling

- What tools exist to allow easy debugging of the application?

Dependencies

- What external libraries does each framework depend upon?

Community

- Who develops the framework, and who backs it?
- What is the size of active users of the framework?

Track record

- Who currently has applications in production built with each framework?
- What is the profile of the applications developed with each framework?

Contributions

- What is the nature of the open source contributions to each framework?

Maturity

- How long has each framework been around?
- How stable is each framework?

Level of abstraction/ structure

- What levels of abstraction around the concept of single-page application does each framework provide?
- What implications do these levels of abstraction have on the development process?

Testability

- How can one go about unit testing an application built using each framework?
- How can one go about end-to-end testing an application built using each framework?
- How testable are applications built using each framework?
- What is the level of importance accorded to testability by the authors of each framework?

The MVC pattern

Model-View-Controller

Model-View-Controller (MVC) is a common software architecture pattern that is popular in web applications.

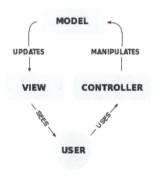

Model-View-Controller interactions

A brief history of single-page applications

Time line:

- One page load per navigation
- Add AJAX
- Web 2.0
- Add MVC patterns
- Single-page applications

In the early days of the web, all web sites made one request to the server, and the server responded with the entire web page to be displayed. Query parameters, cookies, and request headers were just about all a web developer had in his or her toolkit with which interactivity could be accomplished. Web servers did all the grunt work rendering dynamic web pages.

This all changed when Microsoft released IE5 with `XML-HttpRequest`[16], which was a means to send a request to the server and receive the response. This was the first time that this could be done entirely using JavaScript run within a web page. This was a **game changer**.

At first, this was used to simply swap the contents of one `<div>` on the page verbatim with the returned response. Responses were originally HTML fragments to be used as such. This then evolved to XML to represent data that would be parsed by JavaScript in the browser. This went by the name of *Asynchronous JavaScript and XML*, or AJAX[17]. Processing XML in JavaScript was a little unwieldy, and it was much

---

[16]http://en.wikipedia.org/wiki/XMLHttpRequest#Support_in_
Internet_Explorer_versions_5.2C_5.5.2C_and_6

[17]http://en.wikipedia.org/wiki/Ajax_(programming)

easier to transmit JavaScript object literals instead. Douglas Crockford specified the JSON format[18], which gained rapid following. Most AJAX nowadays uses JSON instead of XML, so we should really be calling in *AJAJ* - but the original name stuck.

This disrupted the status quo of one page load per request, and created an explosion in the amount of interactivity possible on a page.

Web developers did exactly that, making their sites very interactive, and thus was born the era of "Web 2.0" web sites. However the client-side JavaScript quite often ended up becoming a tangled mess of unstructured JavaScript - and later on a tangled mess of jQuery - whenever the sites tried to do something complex.

However, server side developers had been using the MVC pattern for some time now, and there was no reason to not do so client side as well. After all, since web sites were no longer thin-clients, JavaScript was being used for more than a few simple updates to the DOM, it was taking over some or all of the core logic of the web site. It thus became pertinent to add

---

[18]http://en.wikipedia.org/wiki/JSON#History

[19]http://en.wikipedia.org/wiki/Web_2.0

some organisation and structure to the JavaScript.

The thing about JavaScript is that it is a strange beast. It has weird quirks that make it behave quite unexpectedly, such as automatic semicolon insertion[20], and an unpredictable equality operator[21]. It also has some really advanced concepts like closures[22] and prototypical inheritance[23], which make it very powerful, but also make attaining true mastery a longer journey. Lastly, it supports both imperative and functional programming paradigms.

With all these actors stewing in the same broth, there were **many many different ways** to accomplish the same things. There were many way to accomplish very similar things. Addy Osmani's JavaScript Design Patterns[24] captures the most popular amongst them. This ultimately resulted in a "Wild West", where everyone did their own thing.

Building complex user interfaces and interfacing with a server is indeed an onerous task. It thus increasingly became important to use a framework when developing web applications. Take a look at the source code of BackboneJs[25], AngularJs[26], or EmberJs[27], to get a feel for how much work would be involved in rolling your own.

There were several frameworks to come out before it did, but BackboneJs was the first to really nail it. It combined the

[20]http://bonsaiden.github.io/JavaScript-Garden/#core.semicolon

[21]http://dorey.github.io/JavaScript-Equality-Table/unified/

[22]https://developer.mozilla.org/en-US/docs/Web/JavaScript/Guide/Closures

[23]https://developer.mozilla.org/en-US/docs/Web/JavaScript/Guide/Inheritance_and_the_prototype_chain

[24]http://addyosmani.com/resources/essentialjsdesignpatterns/book/#designpatternsjavascript

[25]https://github.com/jashkenas/backbone/

[26]https://github.com/angular/angular.js/

[27]https://github.com/emberjs/ember.js/

use of AJAX with MVC patterns in a JavaScript library that allowed front end developers to create a single-page application - an application where every page simply used JavaScript to re-render (most of) the visible page in the client, and none of the requests navigated you away from `index.html` (thus the "single page" in "single page application").

This combination of AJAX and the MVC pattern is the cornerstone of single-page application frameworks. BackboneJs was merely the first of many SPA frameworks to gain widespread popularity. There a currently are plethora of different frameworks[28] looking to take its place. AngularJs and EmberJs are two of them.

---

[28]http://todomvc.com

MVC in single-page application frameworks

Prior to single-page applications, logic for web applications was coded almost entirely on the server - **thin-client, thick-server**. However, with single-page applications, a lot of this logic has been shifted to the client, and the front end developer now needs to be well versed in this pattern.

Most single-page application frameworks are designed around the **MVC** pattern, or variations of it. These variations are usually referred to as MV* frameworks.

Models, views, and controllers form the core parts of most single-page application frameworks, but they optionally may include a few more - templates, routing, and components.

Discussion

We have taken a selective look at the parts of web development history, which have contributed ideas toward - and eventually led to - the rise of single-page applications, and their relationship to the MVC pattern.

In the following articles, we will take a closer look at the MVC pattern, and what working with it is like in AngularJs and EmberJs.

Models

Models in SPAs

Models are objects that represent data that is used by the application. The combination of all models define the **state** of the application.

SPA frameworks, like AngularJs and EmberJs, come with methods to manage and interact with models. They also come with means to sync or map their models with their counterpart models on servers - usually rows in a database via a RESTful[29] API.

---

[29]http://stackoverflow.com/a/671132/194982

Models in AngularJs

Models in AngularJs

AngularJs uses plain ol' JavaScript objects (POJSOs) for models.

```
var myModel = { id: 1, name: 'foo1' };
```

Bam! It was as simple as that - you have got yourself an AngularJs model.

Changing the state of that model is also just as simple, as the syntax is no different from manipulating POJSOs:

```
myModel.name = 'myNewName';
```

Likewise, accessing state is just as easy:

```
myModel.name; // (evaluates to "myNewName")
```

Can it really be that simple? ... Where is the catch?

In order to get any use out of these models, you will need to set them as a property of the $scope variable in a controller, like so:

```
$scope.myModel = myModel;
```

(more on Controllers[30])

... Simple!

However, there are implications when using POJSOs as models, when binding data between the models and views. It means that we need to do dirty checking - keeping a copy of each model in its previous state, and checking for differences at a particular interval. This incurs a heavy performance penalty when models are numerous, or when models get very complex; and working around these limitations requires a in-depth understanding of $scope, $watch, dirty checking, and run loops.

That is a rather advanced topic, and you can read more about the implications of using accessors versus using dirty checking here[31].

That being said, dirty checking is a pretty good value proposition in most cases, as the majority web applications do not have very many models to deal with at once, or have models that are complex enough, to incur the performance penalty.

---

[30]mvc/controllers-angularjs.md

[31]http://blog.bguiz.com/post/57373805814/accessors-vs-dirty-checking-in-javascript-frameworks

Sync'ing AngularJs Models

AngularJs models are just POJSOs, thus when you need to sync them with the server, you are left to implement the means yourself.

The following are the most popular ways to accomplish this, arranged in order of least to most "managed".

- `$http`
  - An AngularJs directive that you would use in a manner similar to `jQuery.ajax`. Use this is you wish to specify interactions on a per request basis, such as when you need the most fine-grained level of control.
- `$resource`
  - An AngularJs directive that wraps `$http`, which allows you to group various `$http` requests together.
- restangular[32]
  - A 3rd party library that makes it easy to sync models with a RESTful API.

We will not go into the syntax for each method here, as each is fairly straight forward to use. The hardest part of this lies in deciding which level of abstraction is appropriate for your application.

As a developer, this is pretty good, as you have several great options to choose from.

---

[32]https://github.com/mgonto/restangular

Models in EmberJs

Models in EmberJs

In EmberJs, the syntax used to express a model is more complex than in AngularJs, as POJSOs may not be used directly, and instead must be "wrapped" using an EmberJs object, like so:

```
var Foo = Ember.Object.extend();
var myModel = Foo.create({ id: 1, name: 'foo1' });
```

Noteworthy here is that we first defined a class for our model, Foo, and then created an instance of that class, myModel. We needed to do this because models in EmberJs are expected to conform to a certain interface, in order to work with the rest of the framework. POJSOs are not going to provide this interface, hence we define a class for our model, before instantiating one.

The most important, and frequently used parts of this interface, are accessing and changing properties:

myModel.set('name', 'newFooName'); changes the state of the model.

myModel.get('name'); reads the state of the model.

A common question asked, is, if AngularJs can use POJ-SOs for models, what is preventing EmberJs from doing the same too? One of the main reasons for this is that it is not possible to create observers for property changes on POJSOs (yet). As such, a wrapper class is used to observe property changes - whenever .get() and .set() get called.

My article on using accessors versus using dirty checking here[33] covers this topic in greater detail. To summarise, however: Wrapper objects with accessors (EmberJs' approach) and dirty checking (AngularJs' approach), are merely different ways to solve the same problem, of observing state changes on models.

---

[33]http://blog.bguiz.com/post/57373805814/accessors-vs-dirty-checking-in-javascript-frameworks

Sync'ing EmberJs Models

The syntax above, was, strictly speaking, not exactly a models, they are merely objects. This general purpose wrapper is sufficient for use as models, provided that you are happy to write your own AJAX for all operations. This article shows one great way to do this[34].

The canonical way to do this, is using Ember Data. Ember Data is essentially an ORM[35] that gives you the tools to define your models in Ember, and synchronise them with your RESTful API back end.

To define a model, we have:

```
var Foo = DS.Model.extend({
    name: DS.attr('string')
});
var myModel = Foo.create({ name: 'foo1' });
```

The primary difference here is:

Instead of `Ember.Object.extend()`, use `DS.Model.extend()`. Also, the attributes that the model is expected to have are defined; except for `id`, which is assumed to exist.

It also provides a means to define relationships between the different model classes:

---

[34]http://eviltrout.com/2013/03/23/ember-without-data.html
[35]https://en.wikipedia.org/wiki/Object-relational_mapping

```
var Foo = DS.Model.extend({
    name: DS.attr('string'),
    bars: DS.hasMany('bar')
});
var Bar = DS.Model.extend({
    name: DS.attr('string'),
    foo: DS.belongsTo('foo')
});
//create or fetch some Bar models
var myModel = Foo.create({
    name: 'foo1',
    bars: [100, 101] //IDs of the Bar models
});
```

Ember Data has a RESTAdapter, which allows you to sync the state of these models with the back end, via a RESTful API. This API must conform to a strict format[36] that is quite similar to JSON API[37]; notably with regards to relationships and side loading.

While this sounds like an everything-included solution, in reality, it is quite likely not be such a smooth ride. The format of the API that Ember Data expects is quite precise, and chances are the existing API that you have make your web application talk to is going to differ, and break your application. Ember Data does provide the ability to customise and even write your own adapters, however, things can get very hairy very quickly - just take a look at this attempt to make embedded instead of side loaded data work, using Ember Data[38].

If your back end is written in Ruby on Rails, however, you

---

[36]http://emberjs.com/guides/models/the-rest-adapter/

[37]http://jsonapi.org/format/

[38]http://mozmonkey.com/2013/12/loading-json-with-embedded-records-into-ember-data-1-0-0-beta/

are in luck, as Ember Data includes an `ActiveModelAdapter`[39] that should simply work out of the box.

For those who are writing applications whose back end is **not** Ruby on Rails, and are not starting from scratch, or are not in a position to change the back end API - which, I suspect, would constitute the majority of all developers - what options are available?

- ~~Ember Data~~
- Ember Model[40]: Follows the same syntax as Ember Data, and written by a member of the core team of EmberJs
- Ember RESTless[41]: Also follows the same syntax as Ember Data
- Ember without Ember Data[42]: Use raw `Ember.Objects` and write everything by hand.

Both Ember Model and Ember RESTless provide good alternatives to Ember Data if you want a "managed" approach, but want more flexibility than Ember Data allows. The Ember without Ember Data approach works well best when your application does not need a "managed" approach at all.

Overall, when it comes to sync'ing models with a server, developers using EmberJs are put in a pretty hard spot. Ember Data is the recommended way to do this, yet it is not yet production ready[43] - and it has been in "1.0.0 beta" for 8 months now[44].

---

[39]http://emberjs.com/api/data/classes/DS.ActiveModelAdapter.html
[40]https://github.com/ebryn/ember-model
[41]https://github.com/endlessinc/ember-restless
[42]http://eviltrout.com/2013/03/23/ember-without-data.html
[43]http://emberjs.com/blog/2014/03/18/the-road-to-ember-data-1-0.html
[44]https://github.com/emberjs/data/releases/tag/v1.0.0-beta

This leaves us to choose from several different 3rd party solutions, and fragments the community in terms of the number of different ways that a particular feature can be implemented.

How this might change with ES6

There is currently a draft proposal in ECMAScript 6[45], the standards specification for the next version of JavaScript, for Object.observe(). This specification calls for native methods on all POJSOs that may be used to observe for changes made to object state.

This ability will turn the issue of wrapper objects with accessors versus dirty checking on its head, as **both of them will no longer be necessary** to listen for changes in models, and to accomplish data-binding between models and views. This article[46] even goes as far as to say

> "Everything you think you know about data binding â€" and every trick MVC libraries are using to pull it off â€" is about to be flipped on its head".

It is pertinent to remember, that while some browsers, as well as NodeJs, have already implemented Object.observe(), it is still under discussion, and is still **presently a proposal**. So actual implementation can and will vary; and adoption across all devices, is still relatively unknown.

---

[45] http://wiki.ecmascript.org/doku.php?id=harmony:observe
[46] http://bocoup.com/weblog/javascript-object-observe/

Discussion

We have taken a look at how to use models, and how to sync them with a server, in both AngularJs and EmberJs. There are quite a few significant differences between them.

As we will soon see, AngularJs and EmberJs have different philosophies regarding opinionation. AngularJs leans towards providing many different ways to accomplish any one task, letting the developer choose which one fits their needs best. Providing multiple ways to do sync models with the server is exactly what you would expect.

EmberJs, on the other hand, leans towards choosing the one best, or *omakase*[47], way of doing a particular task, and requiring all developers to follow that. In most facets of a SPA framework, the EmberJs team has come up with this *omakase* way to do things. However, it appears that they are still figuring out the best way for how to sync models with the server. Having different ways to accomplish this runs orthogonal to this philosophy.

The most significant difference between AngularJs models and EmberJs models, is the mechanism that each framework uses to observe changes on them. The pros and cons of the approach chosen by each framework:

- AngularJs uses dirty checking:
    - Dead simple syntax (identical to POJSOs)
    - Incurs a heavy performance penalty when number of models is large, or when for models are complex
- EmberJs uses wrapper objects with accessors
    - More complex, verbose syntax

---

[47]https://twitter.com/tomdale/status/285821254928322561

- Incurs a much lighter performance penalty when number of models for model complexity becomes large

When the draft specification for `Object.observe()` gets formalised, we will expect all of this to change, as it will obviate the need for both wrapper objects with accessors, and dirty checking.

Models, however, are not very useful on their own. Users cannot interact with them. In order to display models, we need views, the *V* in MVC, and we will be taking a look at them next.

Views and Templates

Views in SPAs

Models, views, and controllers are the *M*, *V* and *C* of MVC. Most SPA frameworks use these concepts to help developers structure and organise their code.

Templates

Almost every SPA framework includes one more feature in the same vein as views: Templates. Templating, strictly speaking, is one of the responsibilities of a view in MVC, however, they are large and complex enough to warrant a discussion on their own. This is because all web applications - both traditional and single page - ultimately need to render HTML, which is a document format.

Templates are essentially files with special syntax that allow the developer to specify simple logic with which to render the HTML. This template typically has two inputs, one static, and the other dynamic. The static inputs to the template are the bits that render HTML without any change in between no matter the context. The dynamic inputs to the template are the bits that render HTML differently based on context.

Similarities

In both AngularJs and EmberJs, the static inputs are pure HTML - write them as you would a regular HTML document. Similarly, in both frameworks, the dynamic inputs are identified as any parts in between {{ and }} (double squiggly brackets). In addition to this, in AngularJs, some dynamic input may be also be specified using ng-* attributes, and any custom designed directives added by the developer.

Templates in AngularJs and EmberJs can thus look very similar. This, however, is a superficial similarity - the underlying approach taken by each is fundamentally different.

Templates are where most of the presentation logic occurs.

Views

So if templates handle all the rendering, what is left for the view to do?

As it turns out, in both AngularJs and EmberJs, the developer will rarely ever have to touch the views. This is because they are "batteries included", taking care of most of the heavy lifting for us:

- Deciding when to render the templates
- Two-way binding
- Event handling/ proxying/ bubbling

This will come as a breath of fresh air for those who have developed web apps using BackboneJs, as it is just one of those tedious things that you will not have to do any more. However, the developer will have to use views when they are doing something more advanced, such as:

- Integrating with a 3rd party library that does not provide a AngularJs or EmberJs wrapper
- Do something specific upon completion of rendering
- Inheriting or using mixins to share code between several views or other classes

We shall take a brief look at views, and then focus on templates.

Views in AngularJs

In AngularJs, you never see any JavaScript for views. Instead, you simply invoke the `ngView` directive in the template.
Any custom view logic must be implemented in the controller
in charge of it.

Views in EmberJs

In EmberJs, you may customise a view in JavaScript. As mentioned above, one reason we would want to do this is to integrate with a 3rd party library that does not necessarily understand Ember.

```
var myFooView = Ember.View.extend({
    didInsertElement: function() {
        this._super.apply(this, arguments);
        var svg = this.$('svg').get()[0];
        d3.select(svg); //do something with d3 and the <svg> \
element
    }
});
```

Here, we have overridden the didInsertElement function on the view, since it gets triggered after the view has rendered its contents, and told it to trigger some manipulation of an element within it once this has happened.

Doing this elsewhere would not have worked, because d3 does not understand **when** it should (or should not) perform its actions within an EmberJs view, since it is unaware of EmberJs.

Templates in AngularJs

Views in AngularJs

Syntax

```
<body ng-controller="FooController">
    <input ng-model="foo" value="bar">
    <button ng-click="changeFoo()">{{buttonText}}</button>
</body>
```

AngularJs uses a DOM-based templating mechanism. This means that the templates **are** the rendered HTML. When the application runs, the elements are first rendered with the **original contents** of the template.

Subsequently, AngularJs kicks in, and traverses the entire DOM tree, looking out for for special decorations, and then modifies the DOM according to these decorations. In fact, if you are quick (or cheat by setting some break points), you will notice a flicker between the two.

The special decorations that it looks out for are:

- Directives
    - Elements or attributes that link to modules known to AngularJs

- – AngularJs comes with several built in directives, and all of them are prefixed with ng-*
  - – The developer may also define his own custom directives. We cover this in components[48].
- Markup
  - – Any part of the markup which appears between double squiggly braces, {{like this}}
  - – AngularJs evaluates the expression within these braces, and substitutes it for the result

AngularJs allows for an extremely expressive syntax to be added to the expressions within the templates, including a limited subset of JavaScript expressions, and filters using a UNIX-style pipe (|) syntax.

---

[48]/components/components-angularjs-directives.html

Templates in EmberJs

Views in EmberJs

Syntax

```
{{input type='text value=model.foo'}}
<button {{action 'changeText'}}>{{model.buttonText}}</button>
```

EmberJs uses a templating language, Handlebars[49]. Its approach is fundamentally different to that of AngularJs', as it uses a string-based templating mechanism, as opposed to a DOM-based templating mechanism. This means that it parses the entire template **beforehand**, and generates a series of functions that contain the static inputs to the templates in-line, and accept parameters for the dynamic inputs to the templates.

That explanation would be awfully hard to follow without context - so here is the compiled function that EmberJs + Handlebars would generate for the template specified above.

---

[49]http://handlebarsjs.com/

```
function anonymous(Handlebars,depth0,helpers,partials,data) {
  this.compilerInfo = [4,'>= 1.0.0'];
  helpers = this.merge(helpers, Ember.Handlebars.helpers); da\
ta = data || {};
  var buffer = '', stack1, hashContexts, hashTypes, options, \
helperMissing=helpers.helperMissing, escapeExpression=this.es\
capeExpression;
  hashContexts = {'type': depth0};
  hashTypes = {'type': "STRING"};
  options = {hash:{
    'type': ("text value=model.foo")
  },contexts:[],types:[],hashContexts:hashContexts,hashTypes:\
hashTypes,data:data};
  data.buffer.push(escapeExpression(((stack1 = helpers.input \
|| depth0.input),stack1 ? stack1.call(depth0, options) : help\
erMissing.call(depth0, "input", options))));
  data.buffer.push("\n<button ");
  hashTypes = {};
  hashContexts = {};
  data.buffer.push(escapeExpression(helpers.action.call(depth\
0, "changeText", {hash:{},contexts:[depth0],types:["STRING"],\
hashContexts:hashContexts,hashTypes:hashTypes,data:data})));
  data.buffer.push(">");
  hashTypes = {};
  hashContexts = {};
  data.buffer.push(escapeExpression(helpers._triageMustache.c\
all(depth0, "model.buttonText", {hash:{},contexts:[depth0],ty\
pes:["ID"],hashContexts:hashContexts,hashTypes:hashTypes,data\
:data})));
  data.buffer.push("</button>\n");
  return buffer;
}
```

Do not worry if that looks like gibberish to you - simply
look at how it alternately does `data.buffer.push("some
string");` and `data.buffer.push(/* some expression */);`.
Those are the **static** and **dynamic** inputs respectively. Ultimately, this function builds a string, and that string is added

to the rendered DOM.

The difference between DOM-based templating mechanisms and string-based templating mechanisms may be thought of as an outside-in approach versus an inside-out approach.

Pros and Cons

The string-based templating mechanism has some pros and cons:

- Pros:
    - Since templates are pre-compiled they render quickly
    - No flickering on screen as first render is already populated with the dynamic values
- Cons:
    - Requires an extra compilation step
    - In order for two-way bindings to work, additional DOM nodes need to be inserted[50] - metamorph `<script>` tags in this case

All of these are pretty minor considerations, except for additional DOM nodes being inserted. Littering the DOM with numerous `<script>` tags makes it quite cluttered and ugly, and makes inspecting it a lot less "fun". It makes one wonder, surely, there must be a better way to do this!

The other implication of this is that two-way binding to element *attributes* is simply not possible, using this syntax. EmberJs gets around this by defining a special alternative syntax, `{{bind-attr}}`.

All this put together makes it feel more like something tacked together, rather than a well engineered, elegant, solution.

---

[50]http://emberjs.com/guides/understanding-ember/keeping-templates-up-to-date/

Separately, the syntax allowed for expression within Handlebars templates is quite restrictive. Properties may only be looked up and output as-is. If any processing or formatting is required, the only way to do this is by defining properties on a controller, or by registering Handlebars helper functions[51].

---

[51]http://emberjs.com/guides/templates/writing-helpers/

Considerations for Designers

Developing a web application using a SPA framework requires skills in both JavaScript programming and HTML + CSS design. Sometimes, these are the same person, but quite often, they are not, and people with different skill sets do collaborate via the same framework.

In fact that is one of the **major advantages** of using any SPA framework: They enforce a structures and patterns for organising code and other assets within the code base for the application, leading to more consistency and easier collaboration when developing in a team.

Templates are where most of the **overlap** happens to be, and thus where the collaboration, between programmers and designers needs to occur.

- In an AngularJs application, the framework lets you put as much logic as you wish right into the template.
- In an EmberJs application, the templating engine, Handlebars, does not allow you to put any logic into the templates. You are forced to extract this into the JavaScript code.

Thus with EmberJs, the decision about where the separation occurs has already been made. However, with AngularJs, the decision on where to to draw the line is left up to the programmers and designers to work out themselves.

Additional Libraries

AngularJs has got a solid templating engine going for it, and thus there is no need to use any additional libraries for rendering.

EmberJs with Handlebars, on the other hand, has an offering that has several drawbacks, and naturally, some have tried to write their own.

The most promising amongst them is a new library, HTMLbars[52], which solves many of the problems mentioned above: It is DOM-aware, supports expressions, supports piping, and does all this without cluttering the DOM with `<script>` tags.

- wycats - on how HTMLbars improves on handlebars[53]
- ebryn - HTMLbars is a DOM-aware handlebars[54]

Unfortunately, HTMLBars is not yet ready, and we still have to use Handlebars for now.

---

[52]https://github.com/tildeio/htmlbars
[53]http://gist.github.com/wycats/8116673
[54]http://talks.erikbryn.com/htmlbars/#/6

Discussion

In both AngularJs and EmberJs, the developer only touches views on the odd occasion. This is because both frameworks have such powerful view classes built in.

Most of the view logic is encapsulated within templates, and this is where developers will spend most of their time. Interestingly, this is also the area where programmers and designers will require the most collaboration.

AngularJs and EmberJs take very different approaches towards templating, with the former using DOM-based templating, and the latter using string-based templating; and thus having a number of big limitations.

We have looked at both the *M* and the *V* in MVC, and next we will take a look at controllers, the which that bind models and views together.

Controllers

Controllers in SPAs

Controllers are the final piece of the MVC puzzle. They are the glue that binds models to views/ templates. Their responsibilities include manipulating models, as well as responding to user interactions on the view.

Now, when these tasks performed separately, these are not particularly interesting. However, their real utility becomes apparent when they interact with both models and views simultaneously. For example, the user might click a button rendered by a view, that triggers an action on the controller, which modifies a model. Then some of the attributes that have changed on the model are bound by the template, and the view is notified of this change, and the relevant section of the DOM is re-rendered.

In this sequence of events, the controller is what sits in between the model and the view, passing the appropriate messages between them, enabling all this to happen.

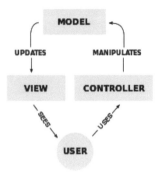

Model-View-Controller interactions

Unlike some of their older SPA framework counterparts, both AngularJs and EmberJs support **two-way** binding. That is:

1. When the model state changes, if any parts of the view are bound to the part of the model that has changed, those parts of the view are re-rendered.
2. When the view state changes, if those parts of the view are bound to parts of the model, those parts of the model are changed.

Controllers in AngularJs

Controllers in AngularJs

Controllers in AngularJs are not, strictly speaking, controllers. In fact AngularJs does not call itself an MVC framework, it calls itself an MVW (model-view-whatever) framework[55] instead. That being said, that si relevant to *academic purist's* point of view. Through a practical lens, AngularJs controllers *are* controllers.

Syntax:

```
angular.module('application', []).controller('FooCtrl', funct\
ion($scope) {
    $scope.someProperty = 'More exclamation marks';
    $scope.someAction = function() {
        $scope.someProperty += '!';
    };
});
```

The $scope object is prototypically inherited[56] from its parent's $scope object - in this case the main application

---

[55]http://plus.google.com/+AngularJS/posts/aZNVhj355G2

[56]https://github.com/angular/angular.js/wiki/Understanding-Scopes#angular-scope-inheritance

object. It is made available through AngularJs' dependency injection framework. This in itself is a fascinating topic that warrants a discussion of its own, as it is a *beautiful* piece of software engineering and architecture. Understanding it lies at core of understanding AngularJs.

Unfortunately, this is not one of the criteria for comparison. I would however, suggest this article on understanding dependency injection[57] for a primer on the basics; and this article on inheritance patterns[58] as further reading.

---

[57]https://github.com/angular/angular.js/wiki/Understanding-Scopes#angular-scope-inheritance

[58]http://blog.mgechev.com/2013/12/18/inheritance-services-controllers-in-angularjs/

Two-way binding in AngularJs

Syntax:

```
<div ng-controller="FooCtrl">
    <button ng-click="someAction()">Press me</button>
    <p>{{someProperty}}</p>
    <input type="text" value="{{someProperty}}">
</div>
```

The template does not do very much. However, it does provide two different ways to modify the same property on the controller's $scope, and thus it serves to succinctly demonstrate two-way binding.

View to Model

When the button is clicked, the controller modifies the model. The template contains a <p> tag whose contents are bound to the model, and the view listens for the change on the model and updates its contents. The template also contains another binding to the same model, in the <input> tag's value attribute, and this is also updated, in a similar manner. Both of these sequences are one way bindings, from model to view.

Model to View

Now, instead of modifying the model, we modify the view instead, by typing into the input field. The model listens for the change in the view, and when the input field is modified, it detects a change and updates the model. The <p> tag, of course, is still bound to the model, and the view listens for a change on the model, and updates its contents, as it did before.

Behind the Scenes

This is two-way binding in action, with the first sequence from view to model, and the second sequence from model back to view.

This magic that happens behind the scenes does **come at a cost** though. As applications become more complex, it becomes more important to know how two-way binding works.

The canonical use case for when this becomes especially important occurs when you have extremely large or complex properties on the $scope - too complex for it to be included in the dirty checking which gets performed in each digest cycle. So instead of storing these properties on the $scope, we store them outside of it, and then manually notify the controller whenever the property has been updated. This is accomplished through $watch[59] and $apply, and using them correctly is contingent upon understanding how two-way binding works, and how it works together with the digest cycle.

These techniques, however, are beyond the scope of this comparison. I would suggest this article on performance tuning[60] as further reading on this technique, and several others.

---

[59]https://docs.angularjs.org/api/ng/type/\protect\char"0024\relaxrootScope.Scope#\protect\char"0024\relaxwatch

[60]http://tech.small-improvements.com/2013/09/10/angularjs-performance-with-large-lists/

Controllers in EmberJs

Controllers in EmberJs

EmberJs controllers conform to the pure MVC definition of them.

Syntax:

```
App.FooController = Ember.Controller.extend({
    someProperty: 'More exclamation marks',
    actions: {
        someAction: function() {
            this.set('someProperty', this.get('someProperty')\
  + '!');
        }
    }
});
```

EmberJs enforces a clean separation between properties and actions within a controller - all actions are grouped into a single hash.

Another things worth pointing out here, is that unlike AngularJs, EmberJs distinguishes between properties set on the controller, and models used by the controller. Models are typically created and passed into a controller, by a Ember.Route object, which we shall take a look at when we

look at routing[61]. This is because there is only one instance
of any controller instantiated, and thus its state does *not* get
reset each time. This is can be confusing when working with
EmberJs for the first time.

Another thing worth noting is that we had to name this
controller `FooController`. In AngularJs, we were free to name
our controller anything we wished to - `BarCtrl` would have
worked just as well as `FooCtrl`. In EmberJs, however, we must
take care to name our controllers - and most other types of
objects - according to the specified naming convention.

This is a common **beginner's gotcha**, and takes some
getting used to. Until then, do not hesitate to refer to the
handy tables, in the naming conventions guide[62] as a reference. A completely customised naming strategy is also possible, by extending (or replacing) EmberJs' default resolver[63].
However, this is often more effort than it is worth, and most
developers will choose to stick to the default resolver.

---

[61]/routing/routes-emberjs.html
[62]http://emberjs.com/guides/concepts/naming-conventions/
[63]http://emberjs.com/api/classes/Ember.DefaultResolver.html

Two-way binding in EmberJs

Syntax:

```
<div>
    <button {{action 'someAction'}}>Exclaim harder</button>
    <p>{{someProperty}}</p>
    {{input type="text' value=someProperty}}
</div>
```

Two-way binding in EmberJs works in a very similar fashion to the way it works in AngularJs - so we will only cover the differences.

The contents of the <p> tag get bound and behave as expected. However, element attributes are problematic - we cannot bind any model values to DOM element attributes using the usual squiggly bracket syntax. The reason for this is that EmberJs inserts <script> tags - one before and one after - each bound section of the template; and of while this works well outside of elements, it does not work too well for attributes.

We need to use the {{bind-attr}} Handlebars helper[64] instead. As this is a very common use case for <input> tags, there is an {{input}} Handlebars helper that does this for us.

The implication of this is that getting two-way binding to work in EmberJs can be more complicated, as there is more syntax to learn.

---

[64]http://emberjs.com/guides/templates/binding-element-attributes/

Imperative versus Declarative Binding

Imperative versus Declarative Syntax in Two-way Binding

In both AngularJs and EmberJs, the syntax used to accomplish two-way binding between models and views is through **declarative syntax** in the templates. We simply **state the what**, properties we want to be bound in the template, and let the framework **figure out the how**, of how to make this happen.

As a developer using either framework, we do not need to figure out the code necessary for this to work.

By contrast, the lack of two-way binding in some other SPA frameworks, such as BackboneJs, means that the developer has to code all the sequences of actions for each property which he/ she wishes to be bound. This is the opposite of the declarative style enabled by AngularJs and EmberJs. It is an imperative style.

Some developers prefer an imperative style of programming, and other developers prefer a declarative style of programming. It is up to you to pick which works best. The vast majority of those developing SPAs however, prefer to use two-way binding, and opt out of it in exceptional cases.

Imperative versus Declarative Syntax in Controllers

Properties on AngularJs controllers are defined imperatively.

Properties on EmberJs controllers can be defined either

imperatively or declaratively.

```
var FoosController = Ember.ArrayController.extend({
    //this is an imperatively defined property
    filterText: '',

    //this is a declaratively defined property
    filteredModel: function() {
        var foos = this.get('model');
        var filterText = this.get('filterText');
        return foos.filter(function(foo) {
            return foo.name.indexOf('filterText') >= 0;
        });
    }.property('model', 'filterText')
});
```

Here EmberJs makes use of `Function.prototype.property()` to define which properties are dependent upon changes on other properties. What EmberJs does behind the scenes is create a Digraph[65], and whenever one of the watched properties changes, traverses the graph to recompute all the other affected properties. Pretty neat!

Noteworthy as well is that we can define computed properties as functions, and when these are referred to elsewhere - either in the templates or a `.get()` on the controller - we simply refer to it by name, and not call the function. In our example, we would use, in the templates:

```
{{#each foo in filteredModel}}
<p>{{foo.name}}</p>
{{/each}}
```

Instead of:

---

[65]http://en.wikipedia.org/wiki/Directed_graph

```
{{#each foo in filteredModel()}}
<p>{{foo.name}}</p>
{{/each}}
```

... which is different from AngularJs. This happens because we have marked that function as being a property. This also serves as a great example of the uniform access principle[66].

In AngularJs, the way to define a computed property is to create a function on the scope. If this property is referenced in a template, it gets called in every digest cycle.

EmberJs' way of specifying computed properties is a lot more succinct than the way it is done in AngularJs. This is also a lot more efficient than AngularJs' approach, as it very neatly side steps the need to recompute them in each digest cycle. While this can also be accomplished in AngularJs using $watch, it is rather nice for the SPA framework to support this out of the box.

---

[66]http://en.wikipedia.org/wiki/Uniform_access_principle

Discussion

When developing applications with BackboneJs[67], the lack of two-way binding capability, or even just any form of automatic binding, was the single biggest drain in productivity. One had to specify in the templates where the models were to be rendered. Subsequently one had to specify listeners for each change on the model, and each change on the view, and write code to handle the change to propagate model changes to the view, and view changes to the model.

This was tedious, but the main problem that this created was not its verbosity. It was that there **always was a chance of oversight**. A chance that one of these change propagations would be missed or forgotten, and lead to much head scratching, and detective work that could have otherwise been avoided, down the road.

What was missing was that BackboneJs did *not* provide a means to define a **single-source of truth** - quite often that the models and views would stray, and get out of sync. With two-way binding, however, the models are indeed the single source of truth, changes to the models made anywhere - be it code within a controller, or user interactions on a view - will be propagated correctly. Getting two-way binding out of the box, as we do with both AngularJs and EmberJs, is a great boon to productivity in developing web applications - I cannot emphasise this enough.

We also took a look at some software engineering paradigms, like imperative versus declarative styles of programming, and the different approaches each framework takes on computed properties; and their impact upon computational efficiency, and ease to work with.

---

[67]http://backbonejs.org/

We have now covered the trifecta of the parts of both
AngularJs and EmberJs that allow us to organise code according to the MVC pattern. Both frameworks excel at supporting
the MVC pattern, providing an excellent infrastructure upon
which to build these.

While MVC lies at the core of developing a single page
application, that is *not all* there is to it. Next we will take a
look at two more crucial parts of each of these frameworks,
routing and components.

Routing

Routing in SPAs

Routing is a mechanism which keeps the **state** of a web application **in sync with its URL**. That is, when its URL changes, the application is· notified that it should transition to a new state. Conversely, when the application transitions to a new state, it updates the URL.

If this sounds like familiar territory, that is because it is! Whenever using a traditional website - where the page refreshes upon each navigation - this is precisely what happens. One page for one URL.

However, when building a single page application, we do not get this by default, and the SPA framework, such as AngularJs or EmberJs, needs to mimic this behaviour without actually changing pages. Before we get into that, however, let us take a step back, to understand why routing is important, and why it continues to be relevant with the advent of single page applications.

- **Expectation**: Routing is what we are already used to when browsing the web; when we navigate to a

different "page" we expect it to have a different URL
- **Browser history**: We expect to be able to use the back and forward buttons while browsing web sites
- **URL sharing**: We have an expectation that by copying the URL from the browser's address bar, and sharing that with others, when they open that URL, they go to a similar state within the web application. Also known as deep linking.
- **Deep linking for packaged applications**: SPAs can be packaged into native applications, using tools such as Phonegap. If a SPA that is packaged within an application supports routing, we can deep link to specific parts of that application.

Thus we can see that it is important for us to support routing, as its absence will detract from the experience and expectations set by existing applications. Before we take a look at how routing is implemented in AngularJs and EmberJs, let us look at URLs in single-page applications

URLs in Single-Page Applications

In single-page applications, the URL is technically always the same, because technically, we are always on the same page. We *pretend* to navigate between different pages, by using JavaScript to replace large sections of the DOM.

However, this would mean that we would lose the benefits of our application being URL-driven. Thankfully there are a couple of different techniques to enable routing to occur.

Hash Fragments

Hash fragments have been around since the early days of the Internet, pre-dating single-page applications, and even JavaScript!

Their usage was very simple though. When you had a web page that was rather long, and you wished to link to a different section on the same page, rather than to a different page, you would do something like this, in your HTML:

```
<a href="#partOfPageManyScrollsAway">
    Clicking here will jump to a part of the page that is man\
y scrolls away
</a>
```

... and somewhere else *in the same document*, we will have:

```
<a name="partOfPageManyScrollsAway">
    You sure got here quickly!
</a>
```

As you may have guessed, clicking on the first `<a>` tag scrolls the second `<a>` tag into view in the browser.

... but that is not all! If you look in the address bar, you will find that the URL has been suffixed with #partOfPage-ManyScrollsAway. When you click on the back button, you go back to where you were originally within the page - the first <a> tag When you click the forward button now, you go back to the second <a> tag again.

You can try this out for yourself! Go to any article on Wikipedia[68] and find citations in line with the text. Many of these are hyperlinks to other <a> tags that are at the bottom of the page, in the list of citations. Click on a few of these in a row, and then use the back and forward buttons.

This was the only way (until recently), where the browser's URL could change without navigating to a different page, **and** forward and back buttons continue working, meaning that browser history was preserved.

Given this, the developers of SPA frameworks decided to use this as the means to store the URL of SPA's current route. That is, as far as the SPA was concerned, its own internal URL **was the hash fragment**. Thus, instead of using words and numbers in hash fragments, they simply used the URL path instead. For example: #/foo/123 or #/bar/123/edit

History API

More recently, however, browsers have started implementing the HTML5 specification. The History API is part of this specification.

It accomplishes something very similar to the hash fragment method, except that the # symbol is no longer present in the URL. That would mean that the end user would be unable to distinguish a single page application from a traditional

---

[68]http://en.wikipedia.org

website - not without firing up the developer's console in a browser anyway.

How the History API[69] accomplishes this is for the server to serve the same file - the index.html of the single page application - for **all** URL paths that match its routes. Subsequently the SPA itself will use the functions in the History API to alter the URL in the address bar, *without* reloading the page. It also also listens for changes in the URL in the address bar, and intercept them *before* a new request is made on the server. This is a little tricky to make work with a single page application, but we do not need to re-invent the wheel, as both AngularJs and EmberJs come with this built in.

This is a clear improvement on the hash fragment method, but there is a catch: not all browsers support it - only the more recent versions of each do. See this chart[70] for the exact browsers and versions.

The History API is an improvement on hash fragments, and we should try to use it where we can, and fall back on hash fragments in other cases.

---

[69]https://developer.mozilla.org/en-US/docs/Web/Guide/API/DOM/Manipulating_the_browser_history

[70]http://caniuse.com/history

Routing and State Machines

State machines are a mathematical concept which has found practical application in a number of things ranging from circuit board design to - you guessed it - routing in single page applications.

There are two main types of state machines that are of interest to us in this context: - finite state machines[71] and - hierarchical state machines[72].

Finite State

A Finite State Machine is one that defines a number of states that an application (the *machine*), can be in. The application is only allowed to be in one state at any point of time. The finite state machine also must define a series of transitions, between one state and another, and the triggering conditions for each of them.

Hierarchical State

A hierarchical state machine is a more **complex version** of a finite state machine. It allows any state to define an entire finite state machine within itself. This may be done recursively, and the end result is a **hierarchy of states**. The same rules regarding states and transitions still apply, however due to the hierarchy, there is one interesting property - there may be more than one state active at a time. Between sibling states in one finite state machine, only one of them may be active at any one point of time, and this still holds true. However, if

---

[71]http://en.wikipedia.org/wiki/Finite-state_machine

[72]http://en.wikipedia.org/wiki/UML_state_machine#Hierarchically_nested_states

this state contains a finite state machine of its own, amongst its child states, one of them is allowed to be active as well.

This is all rather theoretical - what is the application of state machines to single page applications?

Routers are objects that provide routing functionality. Both AngularJs and EmberJs have implemented their routers using state machines.

The router objects store the URL and MVC state for each route in the application in a state machine.

Managing Transitions and Demarcation

The state machine is particularly useful in **managing transitions** between one route and another; in particular, transitions come in handy too add hooks to set up or tear down each state. This would include things like re-rendering a section of the DOM, and adding/ removing listeners. These are key parts of "*plumbing*" type of work that SPA frameworks take care of - the grunt work that happens behind the scenes that would be very tedious (not to mention boring) to do by hand each time. Tedious, but extremely important. It ensures that at any point of time, the state is fully one *or* another, and not in some indeterminate or in-between state that could be hard to recover from.

State machines also make it easier to ensure that the application is **performant**, and does not suffer from things such as memory leaks due to stale event listeners for DOM elements that no longer exist, by demarcating clear entry and exit points where set ups and tear downs need to take place.

Data Retrieval: Callbacks and Promises

When we retrieve data over the network in a single page application, we use AJAX (asynchronous JavaScript and XML). The `XMLHttpRequest` global object, implemented natively in all browsers since IE5, provides the AJAX functions. Using the raw `XMLHttpRequest` object, however, is rather unwieldy, and in order to avoid having to repeating a lot of cruft code each time this needs to be done, we use wrapper objects. AngularJs defines a the `$http` module that fills this role, while EmberJs uses `jQuery`'s AJAX functions.

JavaScript, however, has been single threaded from the get-go, and this poses a fundamental problem for AJAX, due to its asynchronous nature. If we were to block execution of the main JavaScript thread until AJAX requests returned, we would be in for a rather laggy experience on the web. There is thus a need to be be able to execute code asynchronously. There are two ways in which this is solved: callbacks and promises.

Callbacks

Callbacks are the de facto way to run JavaScript asynchronously. As functions are first class objects in JavaScript, we simply pass in a function that should get executed when the asynchronous code returns. That function is referred to as the callback function. In the case of an AJAX request, the callback function would typically parse or do something else with the result returned from the server.

That is pretty neat, but callbacks do have their limitations. Imagine if you wanted to do two tasks that are both asynchronous, but need the second one to execute only *after* the first one has completed. The way to do this would be for the callback function to nest another callback function within itself. If there are three or more things like this, you begin to get some really messy code, characterised by its shape - it looks like a triangle on its side. This known as *"callback hell"*.

Promises

Promises overcome this limitation, by wrapping callback function in promise objects, making it easier to reason about them in sequences or other types of series and groups. The more modern JavaScript libraries have embraced promises as the go to means of dealing with asynchronous code. AngularJs contains its own promise module, $q[73]; and EmberJs has its own promise library, RSVP[74]. Both implementations follow a common specification, the Promises/A+ spec[75], thus their syntax is almost identical.

The next edition of the ECMAScript specification, ES6 Harmony, includes a proposal for concurrency[76], and a draft for generators[77]. The latter, generators, has already been implemented in NodeJs, and is due to come to browsers shortly.

Discussion

We have taken a look at what routing is, and why it continues to be important and relevant in single page applications. We have also looked at the two different ways in which

---

[73]https://docs.angularjs.org/api/ng/service/\protect\char"0024\relaxq
[74]http://emberjs.com/api/classes/Ember.RSVP.html
[75]http://promises-aplus.github.io/promises-spec/
[76]http://wiki.ecmascript.org/doku.php?id=strawman:concurrency
[77]http://wiki.ecmascript.org/doku.php?id=harmony:generators

URLs work in single page applications: hash fragments and the HTML5 History API.

Finally we have taken a look at the concept of state machines, and the crucial role that they play in enabling routing in both AngularJs and EmberJs. These frameworks use different types of state machines - finite and hierarchical. impacts the routing functionality that each can support, and we will examine this in greater detail in the next article.

Routing in AngularJs

Routing in AngularJs

Setting up a router - the object responsible for providing routing capability - is extremely easy in AngularJs:

```
App.config(function($routeProvider) {
    $routeProvider
        .when('/foo', {
            controller: 'FooCtrl',
            templateUrl: 'foo.template.html'
        })
        .when('/bar', {
            controller: 'BarCtrl',
            templateUrl: 'bar.template.html'
        })
        .otherwise({
            redirectTo: '/foo'
        });
});
```

The syntax explains itself (a reliable indicator of great design), but we shall go through it nonetheless.

AngularJs comes with a built-in module, $routeProvider[78], which is in charge of handling routing functionality within the application. This module needs to be configured by the developer.

The $routeProvider module should be configured before the application is initialised, and any other code is run, and therefore this needs to be run during the application's configuration phase[79] of the application's life cycle.

The configuration consists of pairs of routing information, where each pair consists of a URL path, an an object from which an MVC state can be derived. These pairs are passed in by calling .when() on the $routeProvider object. The first parameter being the URL path, and the second parameter an object, which should give AngularJs enough information to derive an MVC state. Typically this would mean pointing to a controller plus a template: a view is generated from a template, and the controller knows how to fetch or construct a model.

---

[78]https://docs.angularjs.org/api/ngRoute/provider/\protect\char"0024\relaxrouteProvider

[79]http://www.angularjshub.com/examples/modules/configurationrunphases/

Finite State Machine in AngularJs' Router

AngularJs' choice of a finite state machine places a significant impact on its routing capability.

In traditional websites, most pages would share common sections, such as the header, footer, navigation menu, and side bars. The more complex ones shared more than that - perhaps the site had several pages dedicated to "Games", and several pages dedicated to "Stories". All the "Games" pages would share a certain section, that would not be present in the "Stories" pages. Similarly, all the "Stories" pages would share a certain section, that would not be present in any of the "Games" pages.

In AngularJs, you may apply the `ngView` directive to a DOM element. When the URL changes, the router determines the new MVC state of the application, and the contents of the `ngView` element are removed, and rendered using the new MVC state.

Since the router is driven by a *finite* state machine under the hood, there can only be one `ngView` rendered within the application at any time. This, of course, precludes us from implementing the scenario above, with the "Games" and "Stories" sections in the scenario described above.

Workarounds

The techniques employed by AngularJs developers to get around this generally fall into in one of two categories:

- Simply repeat the content in the templates, and code in the controllers, for the states with shared content

- Do not use AngularJs' router, and instead use a 3rd party library, ui-router[80], which provides an alternative router that uses a hierarchical state machine.

Some from the AngularJs core team have identified this as a problem, and have drafted this proposal for router design in AngularJs 2.0[81]. It draws inspiration from EmberJs' router, and a few others. Thus, it appears that AngularJs may have support for this in future versions, as there has been a significant community demand for this feature.

---

[80]https://github.com/angular-ui/ui-router
[81]https://groups.google.com/forum/#!topic/angular-dev/mO6jmYhvsMk

Routing in EmberJs

Routing in EmberJs

The EmberJs router, and its associated routing concepts, are significantly more complex than those of AngularJs:

- Supports hierarchical routing, using a hierarchical state machine
- Need to learning naming conventions
- Split of routing responsibility between Router and Route objects

This added complexity makes for a steeper learning curve at first, but pays off afterwards, as it supports a richer set of features.

Syntax:

```
App.Router.map(function() {
    this.resource('foos', function() {
        this.route('foo', { path: '/:foo_id' });
    });
    this.route('bar');
});
```

You might be wondering, but where are the controllers, views, and models named? To make sense of the syntax for the router, it is first necessary to understand EmberJs' philosophy on convention over configuration[82] - and in particular, its naming conventions.

---

[82]http://en.wikipedia.org/wiki/Convention_over_configuration

Convention over Configuration in EmberJs

When you instantiate a new EmberJs application using

```
var App = Ember.Application.create({});
```

The framework will create a `Router` object. It is always named `Router`, no ifs, no buts. This is the first of many **naming conventions** to come!

We then call the `Router.map()` function, and pass in a function that defines a hierarchy of routes, using `this.resource` for routes that have child nodes, and `this.route` for leaf nodes. Both `.resource()` and `.route()` take in a string as their first parameter, and it is the value of this string that EmberJs uses to determine which `Route`, `Controller`, `View`, and template objects it should use. The way it works these out may not be immediately obvious, and this guide serves as a good primer: EmberJs routes guide[83].

The key take away here is that the router object may be thought of as a *king* object in any EmberJs application. Whatever names it uses for its routes determine the names of all the other types of EmberJs objects. When starting out in EmberJs for the first time, this can be incredibly frustrating, as it takes a little getting used to at first, and until then a name that is slightly wrong means that EmberJs does not detect it at all, and simply falls back on using a default or generic implementation of that object. For example naming a controller `FooBarCtrl` instead of `FooBarController`, or naming a template `foo-bar` instead of `foo/bar`.

Know that you are not alone when you are left scratching your head, thinking why your code does not appear to have

---

[83]http://emberjs.com/guides/routing/defining-your-routes/

any effect - instead refer to the routes guide[84] once more
and double check that all the naming conventions have been
adhered to.

Convention over configuration can, and most likely will,
be frustrating to any developer; but only up until the point
that you get used to it. Once past that hurdle, it becomes less
of a hindrance, and more of a boon to productivity, as it does,
by definition, result in having to write less cookie cutter code.

---

[84]http://emberjs.com/guides/routing/defining-your-routes/

Hierarchical State Machine in EmberJs' Router

EmberJs uses a hierarchical state machine in its router implementation. This is evident when inspecting the code that we use to configure the router: In AngularJs all the calls to `.when()` on `$routeProvider` are at the same level. However, in EmberJs, within `.map()` we call `.resource()` and `.route()`, in a **nested manner** - and this is how we configure the hierarchy of states.

The first argument in each `.resource()` and `.route()` is a string, and by default, the URL for any `resource` or `route` is obtained by joining these strings together, in all nodes down the hierarchy. For example:

```javascript
App.Router.map(function() {
    // URL is /foo
    this.resource('foo', function() {
        // URL is /foo/bar
        this.resource('foo.bar', function() {
            // URL is /foo/bar/baz
            this.route('baz');
        });
    });
});
```

While assembling a URL like this is pretty easy - just string concatenation - assembling a **composite MVC state** from a **hierarchy of routes** is not quite that easy. Thankfully, EmberJs does this all for us, however, as developers it is important for us to understand what it does here, so as to use it correctly.

First let us go back to hierarchical state machines. Recall that a hierarchical state machine is a finite state machine, where each state is allowed to contain, within it, an entire finite state machine of its own, and this is allowed to recur to produce multiple levels of hierarchy. Using the following hierarchy as an example:

- info
- games
    - pacman
    - snake
- stories
    - watchmen
    - holes

In this case, the top level finite state machine contains the states info, games, and stories. Both of games and stories contain child finite state machines. Each of these child finite state machines contains two states. Thus both games and stories have two child states.

When switching between top level states, or child states that belong to the same top level state, such as info --> games or games.pacman --> games.snake, we are moving within the same finite state machine, and thus the behaviour is not very complex.

When moving across different finite state machines, however, the process is a little more complex. For example games.pacman --> stories.watchmen means that three different transitions need to occur:

1. exit state games.pacman
2. exit state games and enter state stories
3. enter state stories.pacman

It is important to visualise which states are active, before and after moving between one route and another. EmberJs keeps all the current routes, models, views, templates, and controllers intact, for all the states that **do not change** before and after the transition, tears down those that have been exited from, and sets up those that have been entered.

The developer does not really control this behaviour, but should be aware of when these actions occur, and add code to be executed upon life cycle hooks of each of them when necessary.

- Life cycle Hooks in Views[85]

Controllers are only instantiated once, and their life cycle is managed by Route objects, via:

- model, beforeModel, and afterModel[86],
- setupController, and
- willTransition[87].

Templates, being defined using markup instead of JavaScript, are quite different. For multiple templates to be active at once, in a hierarchy, each template must define where within it its child template should be placed. This is accomplished using the {{outlet}} Handlebars helper. Think of it as telling the template that, when there is a child state that is active on the current route, here is *where* it should be rendered.

---

[85]http://emberjs.com/guides/understanding-ember/the-view-layer/#toc_lifecycle-hooks

[86]http://emberjs.com/guides/routing/preventing-and-retrying-transitions/#toc_aborting-transitions-within-code-model-code-code-beforemodel-code-code-aftermodel-code

[87]http://emberjs.com/guides/routing/preventing-and-retrying-transitions/#toc_preventing-transitions-via-code-willtransition-code

While this is a very simple thing to do, when combined with the power of EmberJs' routing, it can be used to accomplish some types of user interface layouts that would be otherwise hard to do, including the **master-detail pattern**, where the UI displays a list of items, with perhaps just the name in one section of the page (the master), and when each of these is clicked on, all the information about that item is displayed in another section of the page (the detail).

This article by UX Magazine on application screen design[88] lists quite a number of the most common screen layouts in user interfaces. Many of these are only possible when the software rendering them supports the concept of view hierarchies.

I have put together this JsBin to demonstrate hierarchical routing in EmberJs[89], as the short in-line code examples do not really do this justice.

---

[88]http://uxmag.com/articles/rich-internet-application-screen-design
[89]http://jsbin.com/wiyin/4/edit?html,js,output

Routes in EmberJs

Routing in EmberJs is implemented through one `Router` object, and multiple `Route` objects. The primary functions of a `Route` object are to fetch or construct the MVC state of the application when activated. Typically this would involve fetching the model, then passing the model to the controller, and finally telling the view to render its template.

The default implementation of the `Route` object does all of these things, out of the box, without the developer having to do anything. The model however, will simply be empty. In most cases, we want our routes to have models, and fetch these models from a server. Thus, typically the default routes are extended to implement a custom `model` hook.

```
App.FoosRoute = Ember.Route.extend({
    model: function() {
        return [{name: 'f1'}, {name: 'f2'}, {name: 'f3'}];
    }
});
```

That controller always returns an array with hard-coded contents. Useful for stubbing or prototyping, but for applications in production, most likely we will want to retrieve data from an external data source, such as an API server:

```
App.FoosRoute = Ember.Route.extend({
    model: function() {
        var req = Ember.RSVP.resolve(Ember.$.getJSON('/api/fo\
os'));
        return req.then(function resolve(response) {
            return response.foos;
        });
    }
});
```

Here we use jQuery.getJSON()[90] to perform the AJAX
request. AJAX requests, are, of course, asynchronous, and
thus they need to be dealt with using either callbacks or
promises. In EmberJs, the model hook of any route is expected
to return one of two types:

• a plain ol' JavaScript object (POJSO)
• a promise

If a POJSO is returned, EmberJS uses that value immediately. If, on the other hand, a promise is returned, EmberJs
waits until the promise resolves or rejects, and only then does
it continue to initialise the controller and pass the model to it.

Above, we need to wrap the promise-like object returned
by jQuery.getJSON() using Ember.RSVP.resolve() in order
to obtain a promise object that EmberJs knows how to use
correctly. This is yet another stumbling block for anyone
starting with EmberJs, because it quite often means that the
application does not work as expected. It would be great if
this is better documented in EmberJs, or better still, if EmberJs
ships with its own AJAX constructs, as AngularJs does with
its $http modules.

---

[90]http://api.jquery.com/jquery.getjson/

Discussion

Complexity

When it comes to routing, the solution offered by EmberJs is far more powerful than the solution provided by AngularJs. This comes at the expense of complexity - grokking EmberJs' router and route objects can be extremely exasperating for those just starting out, and a lot of that stems from not yet being familiar with the naming system. Once past that hurdle, there is yet more additional complexity inherent in understanding hierarchical state machines and applying that when designing the structure of the routes (and therefore the rest of the application).

AngularJs, on the other hand, provides a much simpler and easier means to define routing for the application. If the application does not require all that added complexity, such as hierarchical views, then this offers a much better output for effort proposition.

Opinionation

Another difference in the routing serves to illustrate the degree of opinionation in each of the frameworks.

In AngularJs, the router defines each of its routes inline, and these routes typically do **not** retrieve the model for the controller. As a result, you see AngularJs developers doing it both ways: Some elect to use the route object's resolve hook[91], whereas others simply defer this to the controllers.

In EmberJs, however, you are *almost* forced to retrieve the model for the controller *within the route objects*, before

---

[91]https://docs.angularjs.org/api/ngRoute/provider/\protect\char"0024\relaxrouteProvider

control is handed over to the controller. (*Almost* because there are ways to work around this).

Components

Components in SPAs

Browsers used to display documents - that is content that had formatted and images, and not very much else. Web pages used to be simply what you could create using a word processor, or see printed on a newspaper, except that it was delivered over the Internet, and displayed on a computer screen.

They are much, much, more than that now! Web pages are interactive, and can respond to the user in ways that a newspaper cannot. Some are so advanced in these types of interactions that the phrase, "web page" no longer seems an apt name - we have taking to calling them *web applications*, or *web apps* now.

The typical things that we create using AngularJs and EmberJs are most certainly not web pages any longer, and fall squarely into the web application category. That being said, the HTML that we implement our web applications with is still very much designed around syntax used to describe *documents*. This makes things tricky for the developer, because over the years, we have created workaround atop workaround to force this document-oriented syntax continue working for us, when what we are really creating is much closer to desktop or mobile software user interfaces.

Thankfully, the standards body that governs HTML recognises this, and is evolving its specifications to keep up with how HTML is being used. The Web Components Specification[92] is a draft specification, which describes a way in which we can create *components* that can be thought of as building blocks. These blocks each contain a HTML template, CSS styles, and JavaScript to describe its behaviour.

Web components, however, are not yet available - but both AngularJs and EmberJs provide their own ways to create components that behave similarly to web components.

---

[92]http://www.w3.org/TR/components-intro/

Components in AngularJs

Components in AngularJs

AngularJs does not provide a direct construct for defining custom components. It does, however, provide a lower-level construct - **directives** - which can be used to create them.

Directives in AngularJs can be used to define the ways in which JavaScript application code interacts with the DOM. We have already seen some of these in action previously: ngModel, ngController, and ngClick. The templates know where code for these directives should be applied, by inspecting DOM elements for the dash-erised versions of directives' names: ng-model, ng-controller, and ng-click.

These are all built-in directives, that ship with AngularJs. You can create your own too, using App.directive()[93], and we will be doing just that to define our own component next: restrict, transclude and isolate scope.

restrict in AngularJs Directives

The bare minimum syntax would be:

---

[93]https://docs.angularjs.org/guide/directive#creating-directives

```
App.directive('fooComponent', function() {
    return {
        templateUrl: 'components/foo.html'
    };
});
```

... and we create a template file at components/foo.html:

```
<div>
    <p>Foo component</p>
</div>
```

In order to use this, we add this to the template:

```
<div foo-component>
</div>
```

All this does is take the template at components/foo.html
and render it within this <div>. This does not look very much
like a component, and lacks a few features that we would
expect of one.

Now we make it a little more useful using restrict:

```
App.directive('fooComponent', function() {
    return {
        restrict: 'E',
        templateUrl: 'components/foo.html'
    };
});
```

Now, we may use it without a <div> tag:

```
<foo-component>
</foo-component>
```

Setting `restrict` to `E` means that AngularJs will allow this directive to be recognised *only* when the directive name is specified as an element. Setting it in an attribute, or as a comment, will no longer work.

As a side note: Beware of the *self-closing tag*! While `<div />` is perfectly legal HTML, `<foo-component />` is **not**, and AngularJs' templating engine will not be able to parse it. Self-closing tags, also known as *void tags*, are **not** allowed when defining custom element tags.

`transclude`

Next, we add `transclude`, like so:

```javascript
App.directive('fooComponent', function() {
    return {
        restrict: 'E',
        transclude: true,
        templateUrl: 'components/foo.html'
    };
});
```

... and we modify the template file at `components/-foo.html`:

```html
<div>
    <div ng-transclude></div>
    <p>Foo component</p>
</div>
```

Do not let the word transclude scare you - I think of it, simply, as *include with an outside transfer*. All it really means is that we can now do this in the DOM:

```
<foo-component>
    <p>Some text included from outside the component</p>
</foo-component>
```

And `<p>` tag containing "Some text included from outside the component", will get rendered within the `<div>` tag with the `ng-transclude` attribute.

Isolate scope

The final step, and likely the most important one, is of scope isolation. In any AngularJs template, the default behaviour is for the scope available on any element to be available on any of its child elements. This is because a child inherits its scope prototypically from its parent's scope.

Scope isolation is about using a directive on a child element, telling it to **use a new scope**. It also allows ways in which select parts of the parent scope may be passed into the child scope. This is a crucial thing to do when building components, as components are supposed to be modular. Thus, if a component is to be useful in a number of different situations, where its parent's scopes may be different, that component should define exactly what it needs in its scope.

The most basic syntax would be:

```
App.directive('fooComponent', function() {
    return {
        restrict: 'E',
        transclude: true,
        scope: true,
        templateUrl: 'components/foo.html'
    };
});
```

Setting scope to true simply indicates that this directive will use its own scope, that is brand new, and thus isolated from its parent's scope. This is not very useful, unless the template for this directive does not need to bind to anything. To create a more useful isolate scope, we use an object:

```
App.directive('fooComponent', function() {
    return {
        restrict: 'E',
        transclude: true,
        scope: {
            bar: '=', //two-way binding
            baz: '@', //attribute binding
        },
        templateUrl: 'components/foo.html'
    };
});
```

... and we use the component like this in the DOM:

```
<foo-component bar=myBar baz="{{myBaz}}">
    <p>Some text included from outside the component</p>
</foo-component>
```

That would mean that the component's scope would contain:

- bar which contains the value of myBar on the parent scope. Whenever the parent scope or the component scope's value changes, the change propagates to the other (two-way binding)

- baz which contains the evaluated value of the expression myBaz on the parent scope. When the value of the parent scope changes, the value in the child scope changes too. However, when the value in the child scope changes, the value in the parent scope will remain the same. This is useful when you know that the child scope should *not* be able to update the parent scope, and therefore do not need to expend the extra effort for two-way binding (it is more computationally expensive).

The most important thing to note here is that by defining isolate scopes, we are effectively **defining the interface** required by the component, which is important when creating modular software.

This has been a very simplified explanation of the concepts of restrict, transclude, and scope isolation in AngularJs directives. These resources cover them in greater depth:

- Creating components with AngularJs[94]
- Understanding Scopes - Directives[95]

---

[94]http://blog.ijasoneverett.com/2013/03/creating-components-with-angular-js/

[95]https://github.com/angular/angular.js/wiki/Understanding-Scopes#-directives

Components in EmberJs

Components in EmberJs

The bare minimum syntax for an EmberJs component would be to simply create a template, according to the naming conventions:

```
{{!-- components/the-foo --}}
<div>
    <p>The Foo</p>
</div>
```

The naming convention is that they be prefixed with `components/`, and the name must contain at least one hyphen (-).

In the DOM, we use a Handlebars helper with the same name as the component:

```
{{the-foo}}
```

All this does however, is render one template within another - not very useful! We want to be able to do the same three things that we did with the AngularJs directive:

- Use elements to represent the component in the DOM (element restriction)
- Display content from the outer template within the component (transclusion)
- Pass in select models or attributes from the outer template to the component (scope and scope isolation)

This is quite easily achieved:

```
{{!-- components/the-foo --}}
<div>
    <p>The Foo. Bar is: {{foo.bar}}</p>
    {{yield}}
</div>
```

... and in the DOM:

```
{{#the-foo foo=model}}
    <p>Some text included from outside the component</p>
{{/the-foo}}
```

In EmberJs, we use a string-based templating language, Handlebars, as opposed to a DOM-based templating language. Thus, we will not ever write, in the DOM, tags names that match the custom component names; instead we use Handlebars helpers, in this case {{the-foo}}.

We display content from the outer template within the component, simply by using the {{yield}} Handlebars helper.

We pass in select attributes from the outer template into the component by defining those attributes within the Handlebars helper invoking the component. This is the only part which requires some custom code.

```
App.TheFooComponent = Ember.Component.extend({
    attributeBindings: ['foo']
});
```

We create an object that extends Ember.Component, according to the naming conventions, and define which properties should be bound by the component using the attribute-Bindings property.

All in all, extremely straight forward, the trickiest part is getting the naming conventions right! The documentation for Ember.Component[96] is a good reference.

---

[96]http://emberjs.com/api/classes/Ember.Component.html

Discussion

In comparing the various aspects of these two SPA frameworks so far, in every single point of comparison, EmberJs' offering has been significantly more complicated - and harder to learn - than its AngularJs counterpart. Components, however, are the odd one out, where the opposite is true.

This is because AngularJs' offering is low-level, and more flexible. In EmberJs, most decisions have been made for you - they can be thought of as "element-restricted, isolate-scoped, transcluded directives"[97].

While AngularJs does not provide a *component* per se, it does provide a means to create them by combining a number of lower level concepts (restrict, transclude and isolate scope) with directives. By combining them together in a certain pattern, one can create components. However, the developer is also free to do something else entirely, and combine them in a different way, or treat some as optional, and this flexibility allows for more specific needs to be catered to.

EmberJs components, on the other hand, provide something very close to the web components specification out of the box, and the developer merely has to extend Ember.Component to get all this functionality.

Both AngularJs and EmberJs have plans to make their frameworks support the web components specifications, when it comes out of draft status. Miško Hevery has written about plans to make web components work seamlessly with AngularJs directives[98]. Yehuda Katz, describes plans for Web

---

[97]http://docs.google.com/presentation/d/
1e0z1pT9JuEh8G5DOtib6XFDHK0GUFtrZrU3IfxJynaA/present?slide=id.
g177e4bd2b_0400

[98]https://groups.google.com/forum/#!msg/polymer-dev/
4RSYaKmbtEk/uYnY3900wpIJ

Components in EmberJs[99], and a concrete plan for "how Ember could adopt semantics similar to web components."

Knowing that both frameworks are aligned with the specifications is good, because applications that are developed with these frameworks will themselves will already be largely compliant with these standards, and gain the benefits inherent from being so, such as future cross-browser support and portability.

---

[99]https://gist.github.com/wycats/9144666b0c606d1838be

Round Up

Models, views, controller, templates, routing, and components are all of the basic building blocks used to develop a single page application. They can be thought of as the core competencies that are provided by single page application frameworks.

Both AngularJs and EmberJs do a remarkable job in providing this functionality, as they cover all bases, and ensure that while developing your web application, you do not need to re-invent the wheel. Neither do you need to worry about conforming to future specifications for the various emerging web standards that we have discuss in this series of articles.

These are just the basics - the foundations - and should serve only to give you a taste for what it is like to develop web applications using each of these frameworks. In my humble opinion, however, these are still the most important things to consider when choosing between these two frameworks.

There are of course, other factors, such as testability, search engine optimisation, developer productivity, level of abstraction, level of opinionation, digest-cycle-specific considerations, and community, which should be considered too.

If you have already formed a strong preference based upon these foundational concepts alone, these higher-order differentiating factors are unlikely to sway you very much.

Contact me on twitter[100] if you have any suggestions or requests for this book.

---

[100]http://twitter.com/bguiz

Fin

The domain of the single page application is a relatively new one, and almost everyone developing them is still learning as they go along. I hope that this exploration of the various trade-offs, syntaxes, philosophies, and other differences between AngularJs and EmberJs has helped you to understand each of these frameworks better, and enabled you to make an informed decision in picking the one that suits your needs, or your app's needs, best.

Editions

The **online edition** of this book is available at angularjs-emberjs-compare.bguiz.com[101].

The **PDF, ePub, and Mobi editions** of this book are available at Leanpub[102].

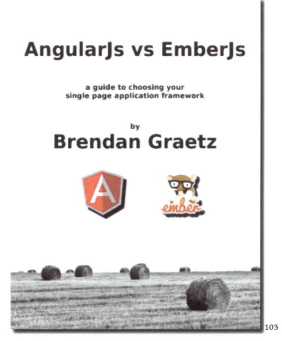

If you liked this book, and wish to support it, please purchase a copy on Leanpub. 10% of proceeds are donated to the Electronic Frontier Foundation[104]. The online edition of

---

[101]http://angularjs-emberjs-compare.bguiz.com

[102]https://leanpub.com/angularjs-emberjs-compare?a=27hVMyWVn46xaZCi6E563X&subID=gitbooke

[103]https://leanpub.com/angularjs-emberjs-compare?a=27hVMyWVn46xaZCi6E563X&subID=gitbookec

[104]https://www.eff.org/

this book is free, and will always remain free.

Author

Hi, I'm Brendan Graetz. You can find me on Twitter[105]:
... and on Github[106]
... and on LinkedIn[107]

I also blog at blog.bguiz.com[108], where you can check out my other writing.

---

[105]https://twitter.com/bguiz
[106]https://github.com/bguiz
[107]https://www.linkedin.com/in/brendangraetz
[108]http://blog.bguiz.com